For Christy Ottaviano, brilliant editor,
and that sums it up! —RKD

To my father, Munetada Yoshikawa, who has been
my biggest and most generous supporter; my family:
Wayne and Kinu; and my mother, Yoko Yoshikawa,
who has been my best friend all my life. I love you. —SY

## About This Book

The illustrations for this book were done
in acrylic, pastel, and paper collage on watercolor
paper. This book was edited by Christy Ottaviano and designed by
Angelie Yap. The production was supervised by Lillian Sun, and the production
editor was Jen Graham. The text was set in Billy, and the display type is Chowderhead.

# What Is Math?

Rebecca Kai Dotlich

illustrated by Sachiko Yoshikawa

Christy Ottaviano Books
LITTLE, BROWN AND COMPANY
New York  Boston

**W**hat is math?
So many things.
It's the age of a tree
counted by rings.

It's a matching game,
it's a blastoff chart.
It's a block of days.
It's a whole, it's a part.

Daily chart

|  | M | Tu | W | Thu | Fri |
|---|---|---|---|---|---|
| 9:00 | Math | Writing | Reading | Gym | Reading |
| 9:45 | Reading | Gym | Reading | Music | Science |
| 10:30 | Recess | Recess | Math | Recess | Recess |
| 11:15 | Lunch | Lunch | Recess | Lunch | Lunch |
| 12:00 | Art | Lunch | Lunch | Reading | Gym |
| 12:45 | Writing | Math | Music | Math | Art |
| 1:30 | Social s. | Reading | Gym | Science | Math |
| 2:30 | M | Science | Writing | Social s. | Writing |
|  |  | Music | Science | | |

Math is five twigs
plus adding one rock.
It's counting gold coins.
A calendar, a clock.

What is math?
It's enough cubbyholes.
It's the number of goldfish
swimming in bowls.

It's counting the eggs
that a lemon cake needs.
It's which weighs more,
the beans or the seeds?

Lemon Cake

...up sugar, 3 tbsp butter, 6 eggs,
4 cups flour, 2 cups milk,
2½ teaspoons of baking powder,
2 tablespoons lemon juice,
1 teaspoons of vanilla extract,
Beat sugar and butter together.
Grease a 9 inch square pan.
Preheat the oven 350 degrees.
Sift flour and baking powder...
Pour in milk... lemon zest and 1...
...lemon... mix... add...

FLOUR

BAKIN
POWD

NET WT 6

What is math?
It's building a house.

It's the pattern of seasons.
The size of a mouse.

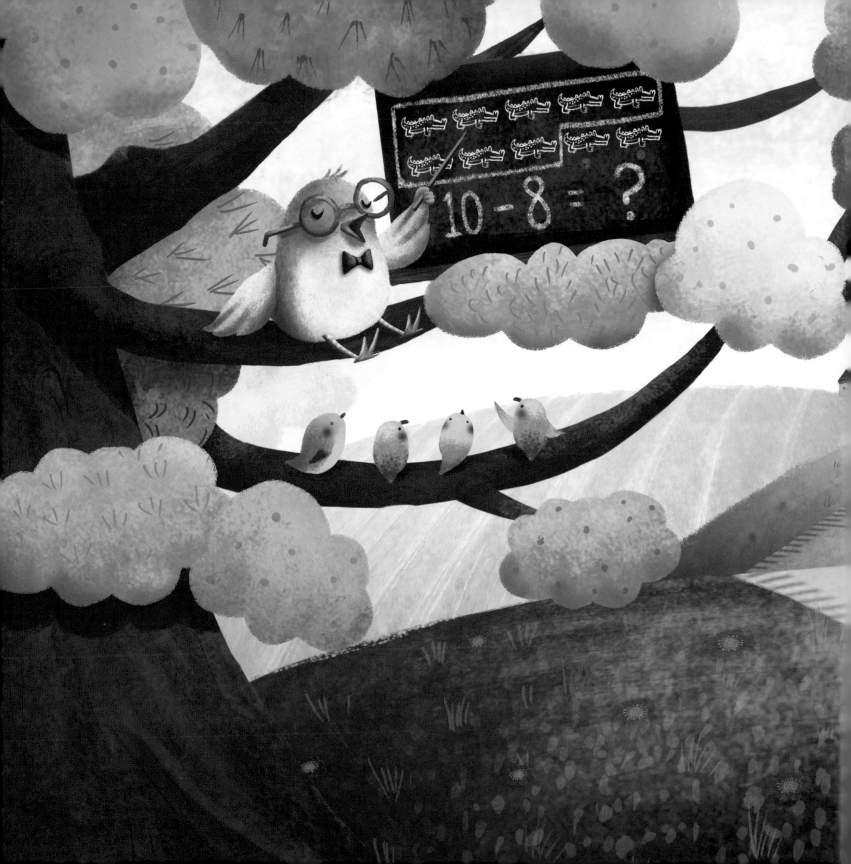

It's the distance you ride
to school, in miles.
It's ten minus eight
equals two crocodiles!

SCHOOL BUS

2 miles

3 miles

1 mile

Bracelets    Lemonade

Math is allowance.
And lemonade stands.
It's sorting the red
and the blue rubber bands.

It's a few bowls of berries.
It's look and compare.
Which group is greater?
The one over there?

TWO dogs were making a spaceship from SIX old tires and FOUR rectangles and then . . .

It's number stories.
It's cubes and squares.
It's rectangles, circles,
and cones in pairs.

It's cutout snowflakes.
A small honeycomb.
It's patterns, and patterns
you see close to home.

It's penny candy.
There's ten in a row.

If you choose them all,
how much will you owe?

It's more than a minute.
It's less than a day.
It's the number of hours
you have left to play.

It's a chart, a graph.
It's how we use tools.
It's a colorful grid
of one hundred spools.

It's schools and skyscrapers,
bridges and roads.
Math figures it out
in numbers and codes.

Our world can be measured
with rulers and strings.

What is math?
So many things!